THEY DIED TOO YOUNG

ELVIS PRESLEY

BY
Melissa Hardinge

||| •PARRAGON• |||

This edition first published by Parragon Books Ltd in 1995

Produced by
Magpie Books Ltd, London

Copyright © Parragon Book Service Ltd 1995
Unit 13–17, Avonbridge Trading Estate, Atlantic Road
Avonmouth, Bristol, BS11 9QD

Illustrations courtesy of: Rex Features

ISBN 0 75250 164 X

A copy of the British Library Cataloguing in Publication
Data is available from the British Library.

Typeset by Hewer Text Composition Services, Edinburgh
Printed in Singapore by Printlink International Co.

THEY DIED TOO YOUNG
Elvis Presley

Humble Beginnings

When Elvis Presley died on 16 August 1977, he was the most successful recording artist in the world. He had achieved 63 gold singles, 26 platinum albums, 37 gold albums, and 18 number 1 hits. He had been awarded three Grammys, and had starred in 33 movies. But his start in life could hardly have been less auspicious.

The Presleys had been down on their luck for generations. Elvis had a great grandmother who bore ten illegitimate children, and a mad Aunt Dixie who lived in an asylum, crazed from syphilis. The family lived in the poorest part of the small town of Tupelo, Mississippi, looked down on by their neighbours for being no-good Southern white trash.

Elvis' father, Vernon Elvis Presley, was an uneducated labourer, unambitious, idle, and having grown up poor, did not expect anything different. He got occasional work driving trucks, but frittered his wages away on drink and gambling. His mother Gladys Love Presley (nee Smith) was part Cherokee Indian, part Jewish, part Scots Irish, who worked as a machine operator at the Tupelo Garment Company until Elvis' birth. She had once had dreams of making something of her life, but the Depression and Vernon's waywardness had put paid to all that. Instead, they were so poor she had to wear rags on her feet instead of shoes, and soon she too began to find that her only escape was in a bottle.

Elvis Aron Presley was born on 8 January 1935 in his parents' tiny two-roomed shack. Gladys was twenty-two and Vernon was eighteen, they had been married for two years, and this was Gladys' first pregnancy.

It was a particularly painful and difficult labour, and Gladys, weak from the loss of blood, first gave birth to a stillborn boy, who was later christened Jesse Garon Presley. Thirty-five minutes later, Elvis Aron arrived.

The family could not afford to bury their dead child, so the local church donated a coffin and a plot of land in the cemetery. Tragically the grave was never marked, and later when Elvis wanted to bring his dead brother to be buried at his Graceland home, he was unable to find him.

Gladys was distraught at her loss, and became inconsolable when she was told she would not be able to have more children. She clung hysterically to her surviving son, not even letting Vernon near him.

The family gilded Jesse's memory. Gladys would use his death to discipline the young Elvis: 'Jesse would never have treated his Mama like that.' And Elvis would always think of Jesse as his other half – he could never be whole until he was reunited with him in the hereafter. 'If only Jesse were here', he would say whenever something good happened.

When Elvis was three, Vernon was arrested for forging a cheque for $100.

During his time in prison, Gladys and Elvis were homeless, and would walk to the benefit office through the snow with bare feet, setting the uncharitable tongues of Tupelo wagging.

Gladys' one consolation was Elvis; she was besotted with her chubby, pretty child with his blond hair and big blue eyes. In Vernon's absence, a powerful bond grew between mother and son, and when Vernon was eventually released from prison eight months later, pleading family hardship, he found his wife haggard, exhausted, and completely unreceptive to him. She even insisted that Elvis slept in their bed.

While Vernon was unlikely to want to better himself and Gladys knew her own lot was probably fixed, she was determined that her only child would have every chance to improve himself: perhaps he would one day have a steady job with a pension, maybe even one day he would be a preacher?

She walked her son to school every day, and made sure they attended church regularly – a Pentecostal chapel with wild euphoric services. Elvis apparently loved going, and would squirm on his mother's knee or run up the aisle whenever the hymns were played.

Gladys was anxious to ensure that her son would have the decency and integrity so lacking in his father. One day eight-year-old Elvis was walking back from school with his cousin, when they passed a farmer selling apples. Determined to get one for Gladys, and knowing he had no money, he sneaked round the back of the truck, and pinched one off the back. But when he presented it to his mother, she marched him all the way back to the farmer, handed the apple back, and made him apologize. Elvis said later that the incident would never have happened had they not been so poor, and it only strengthened his nascent determination to get rich, so he could give his beloved mother everything Vernon had failed to provide.

From the age of ten, Elvis worked to bring in money for the family. There was one period when both his parents were unemployed, and he worked after school, doing odd jobs every evening from 3 pm to 10 pm. For his tenth birthday, Gladys bought him a guitar (the bicycle he wanted was too expensive) and his uncle showed him a few chords. He would sit for hours copying the songs on the radio – everything from the blues and gospel to hillbilly and pop.

The biggest event of the year in the South was the Mississippi–Alabama Fair, and the highlight for the people of Tupelo and the surrounding towns was the talent contest. Gladys persuaded Elvis to enter. Shaking with nerves, he had to stand on a chair to reach the microphone, but his rendition of 'Old Shep' brought the house down and he won the second prize of five dollars. Gladys wept with pride – she said it was the best day of her whole life – and Elvis rather enjoyed his first taste of public approval.

When Elvis was thirteen, the family were forced to move states to Memphis, Tennessee, because Vernon had been caught moonshining (making whisky illegally), and was run out of town by the county sheriff. Elvis was furious at his father for letting them down yet again, this time so publicly, but Vernon promised he would try to get a steady job in Memphis, and the family began to see the move as a fresh start.

Elvis found it difficult to adjust to the bustle of a big city, he missed the country-side of Tupelo, and hated his new school, which was enormous (1,500 pupils). On the first day he walked straight home after Vernon dropped him off. And Gladys would not let him try out for the football team; she said he might get hurt.

Meanwhile there was barely enough money to live on, and the relationship between Vernon and Gladys disinte-grated, as they bickered in their tiny apartment. Elvis helped out doing odd jobs, mowing lawns and delivering milk, and, when things were really bad, he would sell a pint of blood to the local hospital for a few dollars.

He bitterly resented the fact that it seemed to be his responsibility to support the family, not Vernon's. He would run flat out down the street until he wore himself out, or smash the windows of deserted tenement blocks.

In the spring of 1949, they became desperate, and Elvis begged to be allowed to leave school so he could earn more money: but if Gladys and Vernon agreed about anything, it was that their son needed an education, and Gladys continued to walk him to school, until he persuaded her not to. Even then, she followed one block behind.

Eventually they swallowed their pride, applied to the welfare, and were moved to a housing project in a largely black area. This meant that Elvis was once again teased at school, his fellow pupils making comments about him being 'so weird only the niggers will let you live near 'em. Don't get too close – who knows what we might catch!'

But Elvis was used to being an outsider, and spent a lot of time on his own, wandering around downtown Memphis. He would hang around the blues clubs on Beale Street, and at Lansky's where the black musicians bought their flashy clothes, and listen to the gospel choirs in the churches on the black side of town. He dyed his long blond hair black, and lacquered it up like a helmet. He bought second-hand sharp garish clothes – pink shirts with green trousers, polka dots with stripes – and he even wore mascara to cover up his blond eyelashes (Gladys' idea). 'At least it'll be easy to spot me if I get run over', he said.

Elvis the brooding youth

As a young rocker

And he woke up to girls.

First it was a shy crush on one of the usherettes at the cinema where he had a holiday job. Then it was a succession of Saturday night dates he would take to the movies. Gladys hated the idea of sharing her son, and made Elvis feel as guilty as possible when he was just about to go out.

Elvis's first true love was Dixie Locke, who sat opposite him in English class. She was everything Elvis dreamed of, petite, pure and kind; he could not believe a girl like that could be interested in him. He even plucked up enough courage to tell her he lived in the projects, and was convinced she must love him when her only response was to rock him gently in her arms.

With new found confidence, Elvis entered the Humes High senior class variety show. He won, singing a ballad to the open mouths of all his erstwhile detractors in his class.

For the first time Elvis felt invincible. He was going to be a famous singer. He would be able to buy Gladys anything she wanted. And he would marry Dixie.

But when Elvis proposed to her on their senior prom night, Dixie said no. Elvis could not believe it, and spent the next weeks moping around, crying, completely disillusioned. Gladys could hardly disguise her relief.

Sam Phillips
and Colonel Parker

In the summer of 1953 Elvis graduated, the first Presley to finish high school. Still heartbroken, he busied himself with trying to find work, signing up at the unemployment centre. He needed to find a well paid job, because Gladys was confined to her bed with yet another mysterious illness, and Vernon was happy to let Elvis assume the burden of bringing home the daily bread. First he was a factory worker at Precision Tool Company, then he was taken on as a driver for Crown Electric, for $45 a week.

Only working 40 hours a week, Elvis had more free time than he had ever known. He was drawn down to Beale Street and would sit for hours in the smoky clubs, listening to the music and meeting women who were altogether different from his high school sweetheart. He lost his virginity to a woman called Laura he met in a bar. She was the first in a steady stream of one-night stands: he was determined never to let a woman hurt him again.

Elvis' first public performance after high school was at Hernando's Hideaway, a seedy bar where they jeered at his green trousers and pink shirt. Even though he got a bottle thrown at him that night, he persevered, and over the next few months, searched out every amateur night and talent competition in the Memphis area. It was gruelling, depressing, and more than once he came close to quitting.

Late in the summer of 1953, Elvis set foot for the first time in a recording studio. He had seen the sign 'We record anything, anytime, anywhere, $3 one side, $4 two sides' in the window of Sam Phillips' Memphis Recording Service, also the base for the Sun record label. The story goes that Elvis wanted to make a record as a birthday present for his mother. But as his mother's birthday was in April, it seems more likely that he just wanted to hear how he sounded on vinyl.

The studio was very busy that afternoon, and while he was waiting, the receptionist Marion Keisker tried to strike up a conversation with him. 'Who do you sound like?' she asked. 'I don't sound like nobody, ma'am' he replied. Marion was sufficiently interested to stick a tape in a spare machine when it came to his turn. She knew that the owner of Sun Records, Sam Phillips, was looking for a new star, having previously launched the careers of Roy Orbison and Jerry Lee Lewis. He is famously quoted as saying that he knew if he could find a white man who could sing with the sound of a black man, then he could make a billion dollars.

When Marion played him the first tape, he liked it but was not overwhelmed. Apparently he thought nothing more of it until Elvis showed up at the studio again the following January (1954) to make a record for a girlfriend. This time Phillips was at the controls himself, was considerably more impressed, and took a contact number (the rabbi who lived downstairs from the Presleys, who did not have a phone.)

When Elvis returned home from work a couple of weeks later to find a message that Sun Records had called, he immediately assumed it was the receptionist being forward. But when he phoned, to his utter disbelief, it was Sam Phillips who wanted to speak to him.

Apparently Phillips did not necessarily think that Elvis was 'the one', but he needed a singer to record a ballad called 'Without You'. The song had originally been sent to him on a demo tape, and they could not find the singer, an unknown black kid who had just happened to be hanging around the studio.

But Elvis' enthusiasm could not make up for his lack of experience. 'Without You' was a difficult song, and even though they tried it again and again, the results were disastrous. Elvis was mortified, becoming

18

more and more choked with every take. Then, during a break, Phillips asked Elvis what he could sing. He took a deep breath, and gave it everything he had: gospel hymns, blues songs, Dean Martin covers, sometimes a snatch of a chorus, sometimes the whole song.

Phillips decided to give him a second chance, and he introduced him to two musicians: Scotty Moore, a 21 year old guitarist, and Bill Black, a bassist.

Together they experimented and re-hearsed, performing at a couple of clubs, then going back into the studio. None of them really knew the sound they were looking for: it was not regimented Bill Haley country-swing, nor was it straight country, or straight rhythm & blues, or straight pop. Then during a break, on the night of 5 July 1954, Elvis suddenly started

Graceland

The army was good for the image

singing an old country blues track, 'That's all right, Mama', and when the two musicians improvised and joined in, Phillips knew they were on to something. They recorded the track, and put 'Blue Moon of Kentucky' on the B side.

Just two days later, as a favour to Phillips, the biggest Memphis radio station WHBQ agreed to play the record. Elvis was too nervous to listen to it go out, so he tuned his parents' radio for them, and left to go to see a Tony Curtis movie at the local cinema.

Within a week, Sun had received over 5,000 orders for the record. It climbed to number 3 on the local country and western chart, but even though Phillips mailed copies to every big national radio station, it dropped like a stone.

Meanwhile Elvis carried on working at the Crown Electric: although he, Scotty and Bill were doing more nightclub dates, he was reluctant to give up the security of the truck driving job. It was only when Phillips gave him his first royalty cheque for $200, that Elvis finally handed in his keys.

Elvis's first purchases were a dress and a pair of shoes for Gladys. Her feet were far too swollen to fit into the shoes, but she kept them in a plastic bag at the side of her bed, and would look at them every time she passed the door.

As Elvis began to pick up bookings away from home, Phillips impressed upon him the importance of getting a manager. He had the studio and label to run and could no longer give Elvis' career the attention it needed. He suggested a local DJ, Bob

Neal, and even though Vernon was un-impressed, Elvis liked his friendly old boy style. Gladys and Vernon signed the contract on their son's behalf (Elvis was under age), but neither side had a lawyer present. That oversight would cost Neal dearly.

Neal set to work on improving Elvis' image. He arranged for him to have a new Chevrolet on credit, and encouraged him to wear black on stage – the bright colours he thought distracted from his singing. He even had the warts burnt off Elvis' hands.

In January 1955, Elvis released his second record, 'Good Rockin' Tonight', but it was greeted with only modest enthusiasm, and his third single, 'Milkcow Blues' did even less well. It seemed that the novelty of the first record had worn off, and there was starting to be a backlash against 'this animalistic niggerpop' from certain town councils and church meetings. Local DJs got the message, and did not play the records.

In May 1955, twenty-year-old Elvis went on a three-week tour. He looked incredibly handsome, he moved suggestively and for the first time he had his shirt, his jacket, even his shoes ripped off him by screaming girls. Standing in the shadows at these performances was someone who within a year would make this teenage hysteria a national phenomenon.

Colonel Tom Parker was not a Colonel, nor was Tom Parker his real name. He was Dries Van Kuijk, a Dutch illegal immigrant whose conflicting ambitions were to be fantastically rich, but not be traced by the immigration authorities. He was already managing some minor country stars, but when he saw Elvis, he saw potential that Phillips and Neal had missed.

Parker knew that the way to Elvis was through his mother, so he introduced himself to Vernon and Gladys at a club, saying how proud they must be that their son was only months away from huge success. Vernon instantly took to him, and when Parker offered to act as Elvis's consultant, Vernon was all for accepting, even though Gladys said he made her skin crawl. Elvis was not sure what a consultant was, but he desperately wanted his records to break through into the mainstream, and he thought Parker might well be able to help.

White R & B was a revolution waiting to happen. Parker knew that Elvis could be the spearhead, and gradually he set about increasing his control over his

career. Through his connections he got
Elvis bookings at larger venues, and the
next single, 'Baby Let's Play House',
broke through into the national country
music chart. Then Parker made his
move. He took the family out to a posh
restaurant and set about expressing his
concerns that Elvis's present manage-
ment did not have what it took to go
all the way to the top. He said that with
all his connections, he could get Elvis a
record deal with one of the big record
companies inside a month.

The Presleys went home that night and
had a long discussion. Vernon was utterly
convinced that they needed Parker, while
Gladys completely mistrusted him. Elvis
was worried about offending Neal and
Phillips, the people who had first believed
in him. 'If it weren't for Mr Phillips, I'd
still be driving a truck.' But his desire to be

Poster for the film *GI Blues*

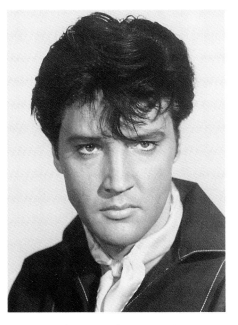

The King of rock 'n' roll

somebody eventually got the better of his qualms: he signed with Parker. It would be a 50:50 split.

Parker's first move was to flog Elvis to the highest bidder. They saw every major record company in New York, and eventually chose the biggest fish in the pond, RCA: Phillips got a $35,000 payoff (which he later invested in a new Memphis business called 'Holiday Inn'), Neal got nothing, (if only he had called in those lawyers) and Elvis received a cheque for $5,000. It was money beyond his wildest dreams. Within weeks, the family moved into their own house, for once on the right side of town, and Vernon and Gladys gave up any attempt at working. At last, Elvis could afford to buy himself suits straight from Lansky's, and even take girls out on dates at Memphis's best restaurants.

'Corrupting the Nation's Youth'

Elvis made his first recordings for RCA in Nashville two days after his 21st birthday in January 1956. 'Heartbreak Hotel' was released two weeks after it was recorded and it rocketed up the *Billboard* charts. 'Don't Be Cruel', 'Hound Dog' and 'I Want You, I Need You, I Love You' soon followed, and the poor only child from the wrong side of town suddenly became the hottest singer in America.

Parker knew the power of the media, and the publicity that could be gained from a bit of healthy controversy, so he paid dozens of girls to faint at Elvis' performances in early 1956. America's youth were only too ready to respond to an idol they could relate to, and his appeal increased in direct proportion to their parents' disapproval. Teenagers, sex and rock and roll were born, and America had never seen anything like it.

Elvis himself was a bit dazed too: 'Every-thing's happened so fast in the past year and a half, I'm all mixed up' he said. The one thing he did appreciate was the importance of the music: he insisted on doing 30 takes of 'Hound Dog' because he wanted it to be perfect. But he was also starting to feel the strain of his double life: on stage, the over-sexed star with his pick of women (he would often sleep with two at once), but plain old mama's boy when he got home.

Gladys had more jewellery and clothes than at any time in her life, but she felt neglected now that Elvis was spending more time away from her than he had ever done. Plus her new neighbours became argumentative when she wanted to build a chicken coop in her back yard. She turned to the bottle with a vengeance.

Meanwhile, the Colonel encouraged his young charge to be utterly dependent on him: he would explain financial arrangements in the most complicated of terms, and when Elvis did not understand, the Colonel would pat him on the back and tell him just to worry about the singing. When the record company was trying to write a sanitized biography of their new star, Elvis confided in the Colonel about

Vernon's disreputable past. Parker reassured Elvis that no-one would find out, and stored up the information for his own use later. There is also the story of a home movie made when Elvis was getting a bit carried away one night with two of his teenage fans. Somehow the tape fell into the Colonel's hands, and whenever in the future Elvis would show signs of independence, Parker would ask Elvis what he thought his mother would think of the tape.

But even though Elvis did not like Parker personally, he certainly liked what was happening to his career: 'Hey, I'll stick with anyone who'll make me rich', he said.

Television was the next step, bringing the raw energy of Elvis' performance straight into the front rooms of middle-class

America. Elvis appeared on *The Dorsey Brothers Stage Show*, singing 'Heartbreak Hotel', and though the performance was well received, he could not wait to leave New York – he was fed up with people teasing him about his 'cute' Southern accent.

As Elvis's career took off, so did the backlash against him. His performance of 'Hound Dog' on the *Milton Berle TV Show* caused outrage, and journalists asked him how he felt about corrupting the morals of the nation's youth. He said that moving to the music came naturally to him, and that he did not see the harm in it. He also hated the phrase on everyone's lips, 'Elvis the Pelvis': 'It's one of the most childish expressions I ever heard coming from an adult', he complained in interviews.

The Colonel had to act quickly to prevent these criticisms gaining momentum, and set about taming his star. First came elocution lessons, and then, in July 1956, he made him appear on the *Steve Allen Show* in a tuxedo, and sing his hit 'Hound Dog' to a basset hound wearing a top hat. Elvis was furious and humiliated, but as usual did as he was told.

Though Elvis was controversial, even disliked, he was news, and by September 1956 it was worth an unprecedented $50,000 to the *Ed Sullivan Show* to have him appear. Some 54 million people tuned into the show that night, an 82 per cent share of the audience. Even though Ed Sullivan told the audience that Elvis was a 'real decent fine boy', CBS insisted he only be filmed from the waist up. Such censorship only served to increase Elvis's notoriety, and that night

Elvis gyrated with everything that was visible.

From television, the next stop had to be movies. Parker negotiated a deal with Hollywood film producer Hal Wallis, who had spotted Elvis's potential at a show in Vegas, and Elvis was cast as Flint Reno in *Love Me Tender*. The film was critically panned, but the audiences loved it and flocked to it. Whether Elvis had any talent as an actor is a moot point, but the fact that he had to make four movies over the next eighteen months hardly gave him any chance to learn the craft. *Love Me Tender* (1956) was followed by *Loving You* (1957), *Jailhouse Rock* (1957) and *King Creole* (1958), all tapping into the poor boy makes good mythology that was Elvis' own story.

The Colonel was not interested in high art – he wanted to see results from his time and commitment. Even though Elvis was offered parts in movies playing opposite Burt Lancaster and Tony Curtis, Parker was happier to accept scripts where there was no doubt who was the star. This related to Elvis' records too: there was little choice of material, because Parker had tied Elvis to singing songs from one particular publishing house. Parker also had no qualms about approving as 'official' Elvis merchandise everything from tacky stuffed hound dogs to pyjamas, without any regard to their quality.

The Draft

Elvis did not take easily to Hollywood. He fell desperately in love with his first co-star Debra Paget, then with another young starlet, Natalie Wood. Also his parents had joined him in Los Angeles, and even though Vernon had no problem with going off sightseeing, Gladys remained stubbornly at Elvis' side, even on the set. This meant that Elvis' usual recreational activities with women had to be curtailed, and he spent long hours cooped up in his hotel room, driving room service crazy

With some of the cast of *Blue Hawaii.*

Elvis and Priscilla

with orders of peanut butter sandwiches and ice-cream in the middle of the night.

When Elvis popped home between his movies, Las Vegas appearances and TV shows, his local celebrity and the crush of fans waiting at the gates of his house made him review his living arrangements. First he hired an old school friend, Red West, as a bodyguard, then he set about finding the family a new home.

Graceland was in a wide leafy street in an area of Memphis called White Haven. The property had fourteen rooms and enough space in the grounds for Gladys to have chickens without the neighbours complaining. Such a home, costing $100,000, was suitable for rich businessmen and diplomats – not bad for Southern white trash. He moved the whole family in July 1957, plus his Grandma Minnie

Mae, some cousins and friends for good measure. Graceland represented everything he had aspired to: he even had the outside repainted so that his Memphis neighbours could see it glowing in the dark.

Red became Elvis' constant companion, and soon there was a group of men, some on the pay-roll, with whom he would hang out. Elvis had never been in a gang before – he had always been the outsider, and he relished his role as ringleader. When he was at home he would hire out the local amusement park for the evening, or the skating rink for $75, and would stay up until dawn with his cronies and their dates. He felt happier when he was with his entourage, and rarely ventured outside Graceland without company. He would go out with Red, looking for dates, and would try to find somewhere to make his conquest – he could not take a girl back to Graceland in case Gladys overheard, and he would always make sure he was back by dawn.

The first Christmas at Graceland was a lavish affair. Elvis even got up at noon (early by his standards) in honour of the celebration. He showered everyone with presents, lit up Graceland like a Christmas tree and swigged champagne by the bottle. It would the last truly happy family holiday.

Elvis was now dating a Memphis television presenter, Anita Wood, though of course he continued his nocturnal jaunts. As she was a celebrity in her own right, they had a natural understanding, and Vernon in particular thought his son should make their relationship permanent. But early in 1958, when Elvis was watching her on TV, he suddenly saw a close-up of a ring on her hand – a ring he had given her the week before. Elvis flew into a rage, screaming that she was only interested in him for his money. This was a frequent complaint: Elvis loved to be generous, but he was always suspicious that people were only friendly because of his success. He was proud when his old classmates would call on him, and was only too pleased to show off the house, but when they had gone he would berate them, saying that when he had been in their class at school they would have nothing to do with him.

1958 was a whirlwind of recording commitments and concerts. But in March, midway through filming his fourth movie, the bombshell dropped. The Colonel rang to say that Elvis had been drafted into the army. Elvis just could not believe it and had a panic attack, hurling furniture

The smouldering looks that won a
million hearts

Just one of Elvis's Cadillacs

out of the window of the expensive Beverly Hills hotel where he was staying. He thought it was the Presley curse, coming once again when things were going so well.

Elvis was frantic at the thought of being away from the music scene for two whole years – what if everyone forgot about him and he had to go back to playing small-town clubs on his return? The Colonel reassured him that they had a movie and several singles in the can, and that maybe absence would make the teenage hearts clamour for him even more on his return.

Elvis left for Fort Hood training camp in Texas, getting his famous black 'DA' haircut shorn in full view of the cameras. The family followed two weeks later to a nearby house in Killeen – not living on base was the one concession Elvis was allowed.

Elvis hated the army – he had always hated being told what to do, and he missed his music and his women. His body ached from the arduous workouts and long hours, and he felt a constant pressure not to make a fool of himself in front of the other soldiers.

Meanwhile, the heat in Texas was getting to Gladys, her skin had turned yellow, and after a couple of months, the family were so concerned about her health that Vernon agreed to take her back to Memphis to see a trusted doctor. While Elvis was fearful for her, he was secretly relieved that she was going home, because it meant he could invite in some of the pretty young fans who hung around outside the house.

Gladys was diagnosed as having hepatitis, and was kept in the Memphis City

Methodist Hospital for a few days, where Elvis called her constantly. Though she was only forty-five, she was in very poor health, overweight, with a swollen liver from her years of drinking. She did not respond to the drugs, and her condition deteriorated so much that Vernon arranged for Elvis to have compassionate leave to come and see her. For once Elvis overcame his fear of flying and rushed to be with her. He was shocked by his mother's appearance, but Gladys insisted that he go home to Graceland to get some rest before coming back to see her the next morning. He went out, hung out with some friends, and then went to his room with Anita.

Gladys died in the middle of the night of 14 August 1958. It was Vernon who broke the news to Elvis, who froze with the shock, sobbing, inconsolable, and furious with himself that he had not stayed at the hospital to be with her at the end.

As the news of her death broke, a huge crowd gathered outside Graceland, and there were hundreds of messages of condolence. Even Dixie, Elvis' first love, showed up at the house, and he just hugged and hugged her. He found no comfort with Anita – he felt guilty that he had been in bed with her when Gladys was taking her last breaths.

The funeral on 16 August was the worst day of Elvis' life. When the attendants came to take the body away (it had been laid out in the music room) Elvis leapt on top of the coffin crying uncontrollably 'Don't leave me mama. I did everything for you. I'll do better this time, just let me try.'

Gladys's death fundamentally changed Elvis. He never forgave himself for letting her down, and he never forgave her for leaving him and going to Jesse, her favourite son. The main focus of his life was gone, and from that point on, he was on a collision course with disaster.

The day after the funeral he had to return to Texas. To dull the pain, he now surrounded himself with people. Whereas before he had not wanted to befriend his fellow officers, he now began to invite them over for meals and drinking, seeking out those who would cater to his every whim. He began to have trouble sleeping, and would have people on guard to make sure he did not sleepwalk out of the house. And his sexual activities became increasingly strange. He would get up early in the morning, and go for drives to look at women's underwear drying on washing lines. He would indulge in bizarre sex games with his conquests, and developed a notion that a woman could not be sexy if she had given birth. He refused to go to bed without company, and would even rather his male cousin slept next to him than be alone.

In September 1958, Elvis was shipped with his division to Bad Nauheim in West Germany. He was pleasantly surprised that his fame preceded him, and that German fans allowed him a little more privacy than their American counterparts. He brought Vernon, Red West and Grandma Minnie Mae over, and they moved into a comfortable three bedroomed house, with a piano, television sets, and fridges full of hamburgers.

Back in the United States, the Colonel worked hard to keep Elvis' career alive.

Elvis and Priscilla were married in May 1967

The new-look Elvis in the rhinestone suit

He ran Elvis Presley competitions, where the prize was visiting Elvis in Germany, and sanctioned a 'fanzine' called *Elvis Monthly*. Both the *Loving You* and *King Creole* albums went platinum, and singles like 'One Night', 'Wear My Ring around Your Neck' and 'Hard Headed Woman' went straight into the top ten. Elvis' recording career was now so strong that the 1959 edition of the *Guinness Book of World Records* listed him as overtaking Bing Crosby as the most successful singer of all time.

In Germany, a thousand fan letters would arrive at the local post office every day. Meanwhile Elvis busied himself with sampling German nightlife, and even flew some of his 'Memphis Mafia' over for excursions to Paris and Munich. Then he met Priscilla.

Priscilla Beaulieu was the daughter of an air force captain, and she was introduced to Elvis at a party at his house: 'Well, what have we here?' he said. One of his friends had spotted her in a café and thought that Elvis might like her. Her parents had only allowed her to go when her father realized he knew the commanding officer of the man concerned.

Priscilla knew who Elvis was. Like every other fan she had bought his records and watched him on the television. When they were introduced, she was so nervous she could hardly speak, but her reserve attracted him, and she was invited back.

What struck Elvis was the resemblance he thought she bore to photographs of the young Gladys. He thought that Jesse had sent Gladys back to him in the form of

Priscilla, and almost immediately he put her right up there on the pedestal next to his mother. He liked the fact that she was only fourteen – pure and untainted, unlike those other women who threw themselves at him and were therefore worthless.

Elvis began to want to see Priscilla all the time. But her parents insisted that they meet him before they were prepared to let this happen. Elvis dressed up in his uniform for the occasion and charmed the Beaulieus with his lovely manners. They agreed that the couple could carry on seeing each other if Elvis promised he would drop Priscilla off personally after each date. Elvis agreed.

In the few remaining months of Elvis' service they saw each other practically every night. Priscilla found it hard to reconcile these hours with her school work, but Elvis gave her small white pills to help her keep awake in class.

Elvis returned home to Memphis on 2 March 1960, and was discharged from the army three days later. Priscilla accompanied him to the airport, and later the papers were full of the story of the girl he left behind. Priscilla declined to be flown over to the States to appear on television shows, and tried to be evasive about her age when nosy journalists became too curious.

Priscilla

Elvis had not been forgotten while he was away. He was besieged by fans at the airport, and the Colonel drew up a busy schedule for him, with the intention of plunging him straight back into the spotlight. Plans were made for the next movie (hardly surprisingly, *G.I. Blues*) Vegas wanted him for a concert stint, and Elvis could hardly wait to get started. But events at home put a dampener on the triumphant return he had been looking forward to.

Vernon announced to Elvis that he was in love with Dee Stanley, a pretty blonde woman 20 years his junior, and he planned to marry her after her divorce from her present husband was finalized. Elvis was outraged: he had often not seen eye to eye with his father, but this was the ultimate betrayal. He himself had not begun to come to terms with the death of his mother: he was shocked that his father could even contemplate another woman. He refused to go to their wedding, and when Vernon moved Dee into Graceland, he kept out of their way as much as he could, throwing himself into his work.

However, he quickly became disillusioned with that too. He thought the *G.I. Blues* script was terrible, and could not believe the cynicism of the studio in wanting to cash in on his time in service. It seemed that the aim of the film was to make

By 1977, Elvis was becoming increasingly depressed

The memorial at Graceland

soldiering seem fun, and hence Elvis was to be the patriotic all-American ideal. It was a far cry from the scandalous rebel that American teenagers had taken to their hearts.

And when he went back into the studio in Nashville, he found that the songs that RCA wanted him to record were disappointing, middle of the road ballads. 'Stuck on You', 'Are You Lonesome Tonight?' and 'It's Now or Never' were all massive hits, but could hardly be described as rock and roll, and sections of the press began to criticize him for cashing in on his success. His appearance on a Frank Sinatra TV special, in his uniform, and then a tuxedo, confirmed these suspicions: meanwhile Sinatra threatened 'his health' if he did not leave his girlfriend Juliet Prowse alone (Juliet was Elvis's co-star in *G.I. Blues*). Elvis expressed his concerns to Parker, but the Colonel was adamant: Elvis had to do the work to re-establish himself on the American music scene. Again Elvis passively agreed.

Over the next nine years, Elvis made 26 films. The most memorable of these were *Blue Hawaii* (1961) with Angela Lansbury, *Girls! Girls! Girls!*(1962), *Viva Las Vegas*(1964) with Ann-Margret, and *A Change of Habit*(1969) with Mary Tyler Moore. Elvis hated them all without exception. He may have been paid a million dollars a movie, but this left no spare money for the sets, good directors or worthy actors, and he felt embarrassed by the corny scripts and painful plotlines. But the Colonel was happy because Elvis was Hollywood's highest paid star; the studio was happy because not one of the movies made a loss; and RCA were happy because they could release an album off the back of each movie.

At home in 1962, Elvis felt isolated, restless and moody. He moved more cronies into Graceland, and would keep them busy with errands at all hours of the day and night. He gorged himself on junk food (then starving himself before each movie), and gobbled pills like they were sweets. He was angry with Gladys for leaving him, angry with Vernon and Dee, angry with his hangers-on for sponging off him.

There became only one way out of his depression. He sent for Priscilla. It was nearly two years since he had left Germany, Priscilla was now sixteen, and after an almighty battle with her parents to let her go, she arrived, petrified that Elvis might find fault with her: she had, after all, put on five pounds. But Elvis thought she was perfect, especially when she confirmed to him that she was still a virgin. He took her shopping, and dressed her up in the latest fashions. But he still did not sleep with her; he wanted to keep the promise he had made to her father when he had agreed to the visit.

It went so well that she was invited back for Christmas. He gave her a poodle puppy and she gave him a cigarette case that played *Love Me Tender*. The whole house seemed to be uplifted by her laughter, and Elvis was briefly transformed into the Elvis of old. He decided that he was not going to let her go back to Germany, and he phoned her parents on New Year's Day 1963.

The deal they struck was that Priscilla *would* return to Germany to finish her school year. She would then move to

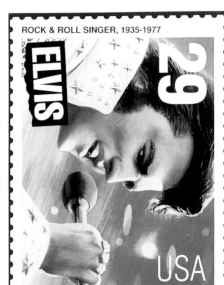

ROCK & ROLL SINGER, 1935-1977

ELVIS

29

USA

An Elvis memorial stamp